My First Sticker Book

Things That Go

Licensed exclusively to Top That Publishing Ltd
Tide Mill Way, Woodbridge, Suffolk, IP12 1AP, UK
www.topthatpublishing.com
Copyright © 2016 Tide Mill Media
All rights reserved
2 4 6 8 9 7 5 3
Manufactured in China

Choo, choo!

The train station is a busy place. Add more engines, a sweeper and baggage carriers — the passengers are waiting!

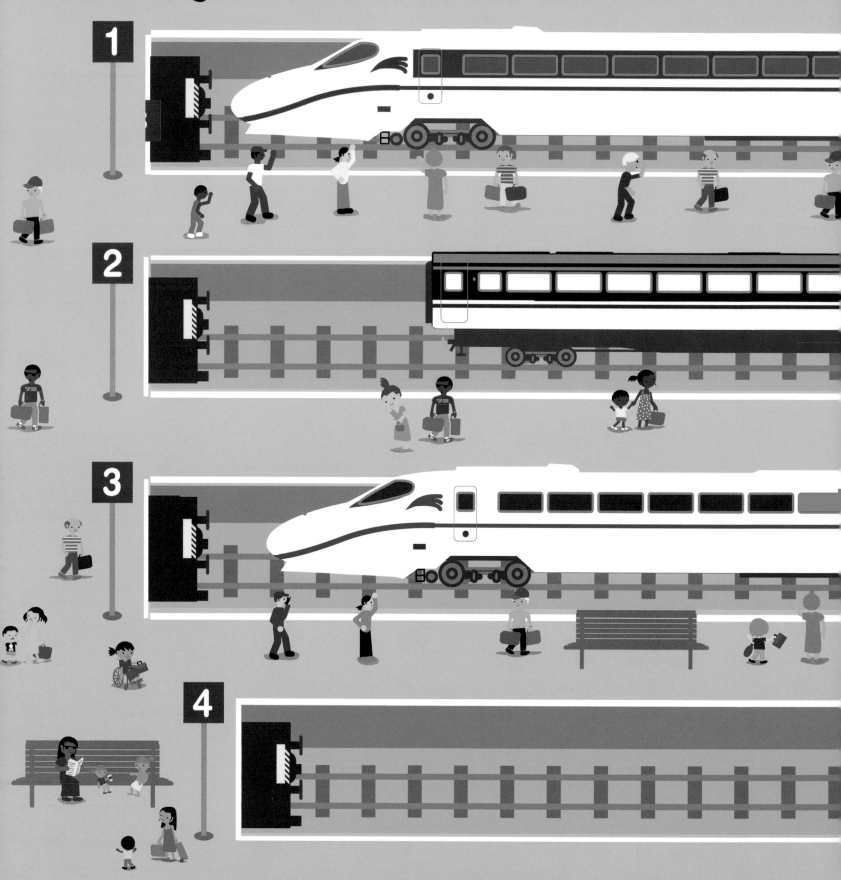

Toot, toot!

This container ship is being loaded with cargo. Add more containers, ships and a lorry to the scene.

Chugga, chugga!

Big machines dig, lift and load at the building site!
Add diggers, dumpers and a crane to the scene.

Vroom, vroom!

3 ... 2 ... 1 ... Go, go, go! Which fast car will win the race? Pick and stick the winner!

Zoom, zoom!

Place aeroplanes onto the busy airport scene so that people can go on holiday.

Beep, beep!

There are lots of cars in the big city.
Add more traffic to the busy road.

Whoosh, whoosh!

Finish the colourful scene by sticking more hot-air balloons in the sky.

Brum, brum!

These off-road cars are big and tough!
Find some more muddy vehicles.

Eeeooo, eeeooo!

There's been an accident. Rush the emergency vehicles to the scene!

Clickety-clack!

It's time to load up the trains with cargo. Add an engine and more freight to the busy yard.

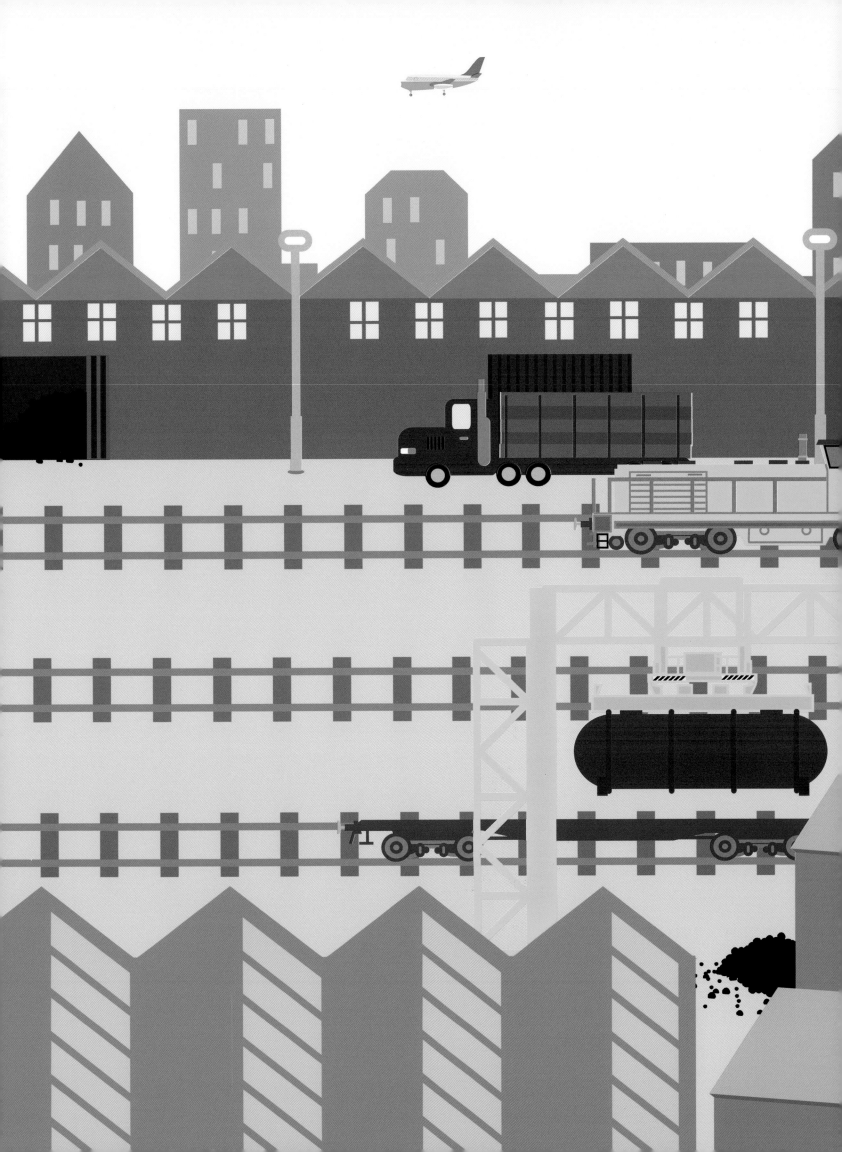

All aboard! Add more buses to take people shopping, to work and school.

Rumble, rumble!

It's harvest time on the farm. Add farm vehicles to cut and load the crops.

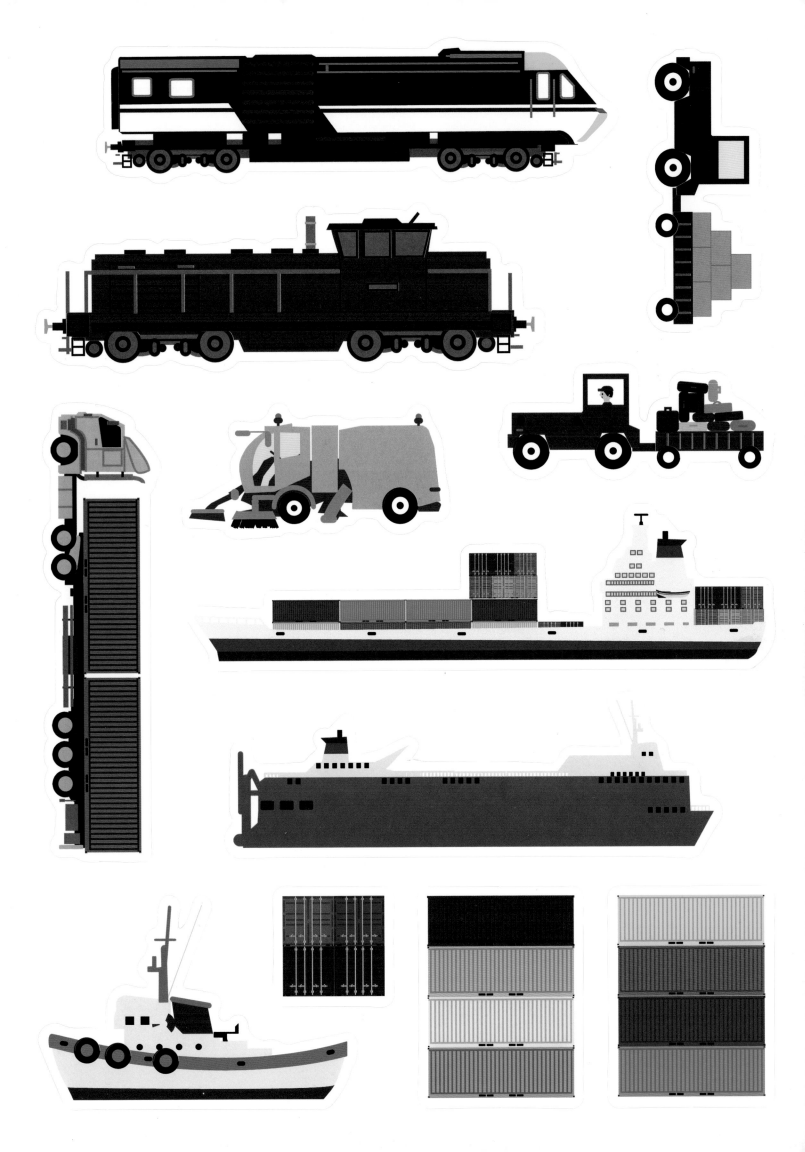

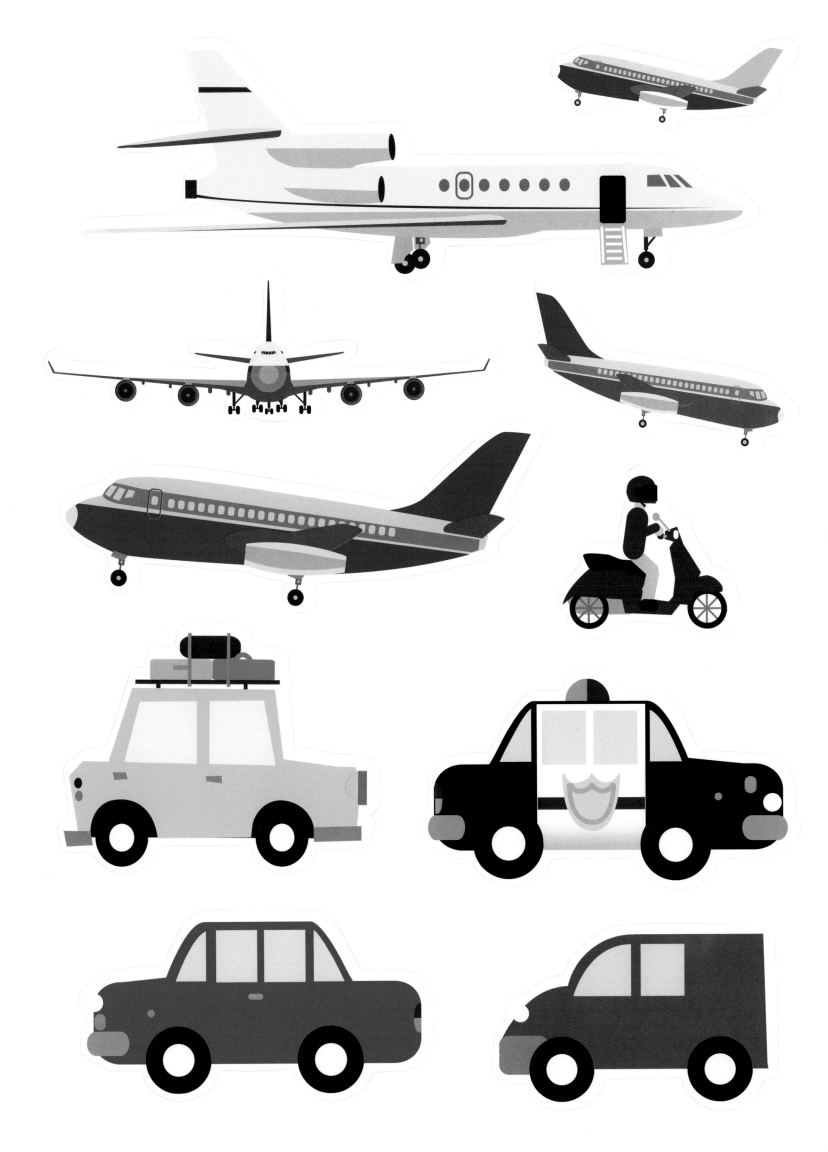

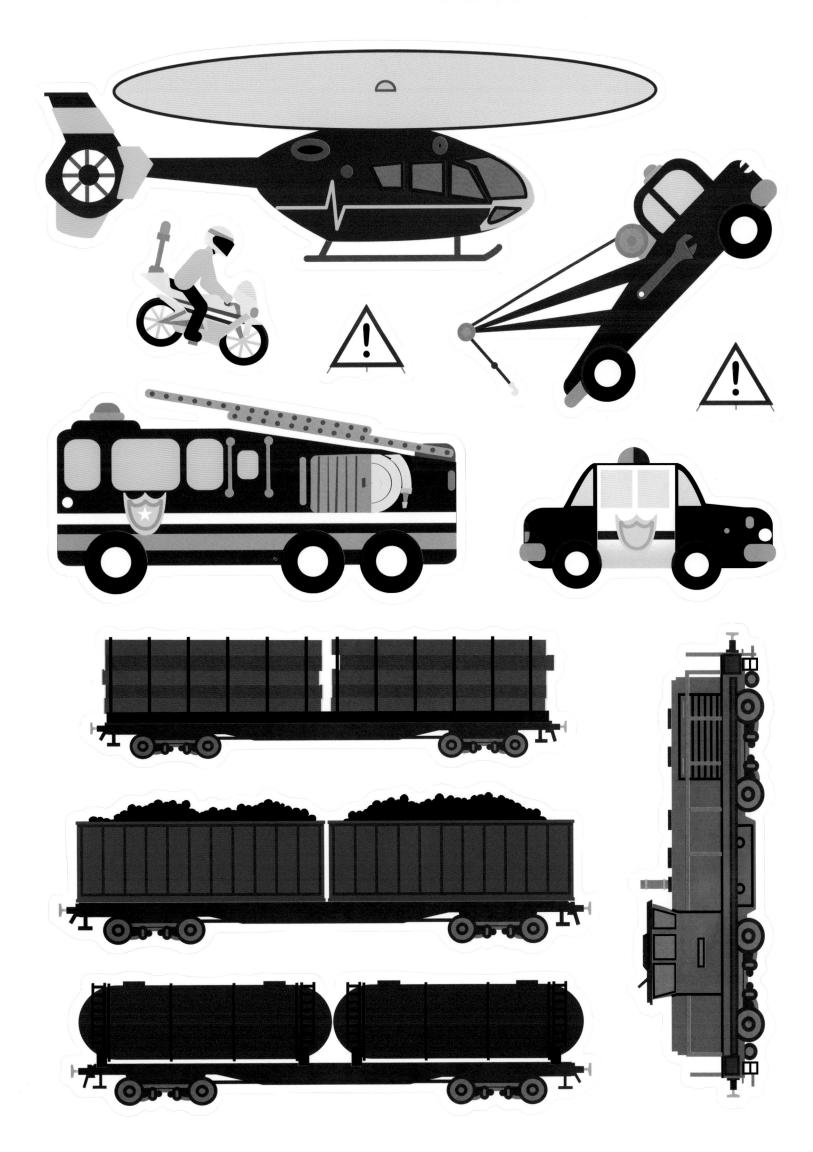

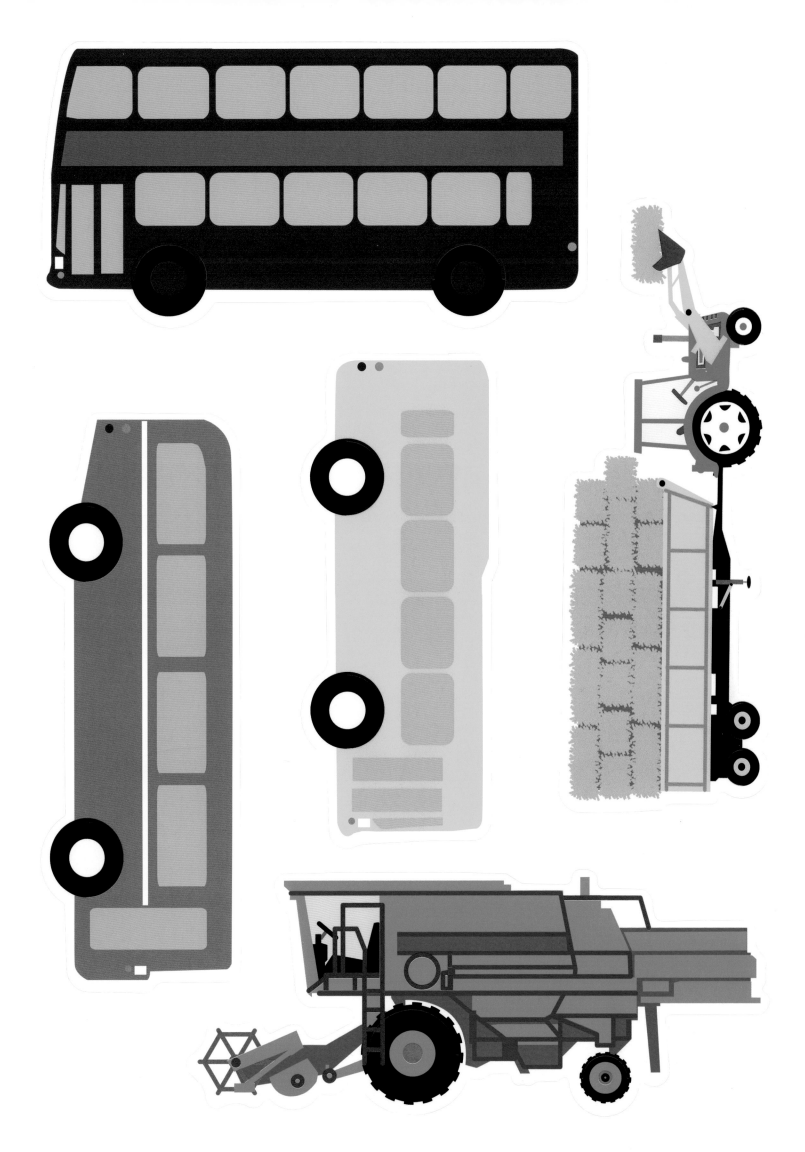